3 1540 00267 3802

Published by Creative Education
123 South Broad Street, Mankato, Minnesota 56001

Creative Education is an imprint of The Creative Company.

Designed by Stephanie Blumenthal
Production design by Melinda Belter
Art direction by Rita Marshall

Photographs by Alamy (AA World Travel Library, ACE STOCK LIMITED, Douglas Armand, BL Images Ltd, Bora, Covalart Photographic, Directphoto.org, Chad Ehlers, Fotofacade, FrenchStockOne, Dennis Hallinan, Xavier HENRI, Frank Herholdt, D. Hurst, Andre Jenny, Terrance Klassen, Mary Evans Picture Library, Andrew Morse, nagelestock.com, POPPERFOTO, Profimedia.CZ.s.r.o., Robert Harding Picture Library Ltd, SCPhotos, Frantisek Staud, StockAbcd) Art Resource, NY (Erich Lessing), Design Maps Inc., Getty Images (General Photographic Agency, Three Lions), The Granger Collection, NY (pages 8, 10, 16)

Printed in the United States of America

Library of Congress Cataloging-in-Publication Data
LeBoutillier, Nate.
Eiffel Tower / by Nate LeBoutillier.
p. cm. — (Modern wonders of the world)
Includes index.
ISBN-13: 978-1-58341-438-5
1. Tour Eiffel (Paris, France)—Juvenile literature. 2. Paris (France)—Buildings, structures, etc.—
Juvenile literature. I. Title. II. Series.

NA2930.L38 2006   725'.97'0944361—dc22   2005050805

First edition

2 4 6 8 9 7 5 3 1

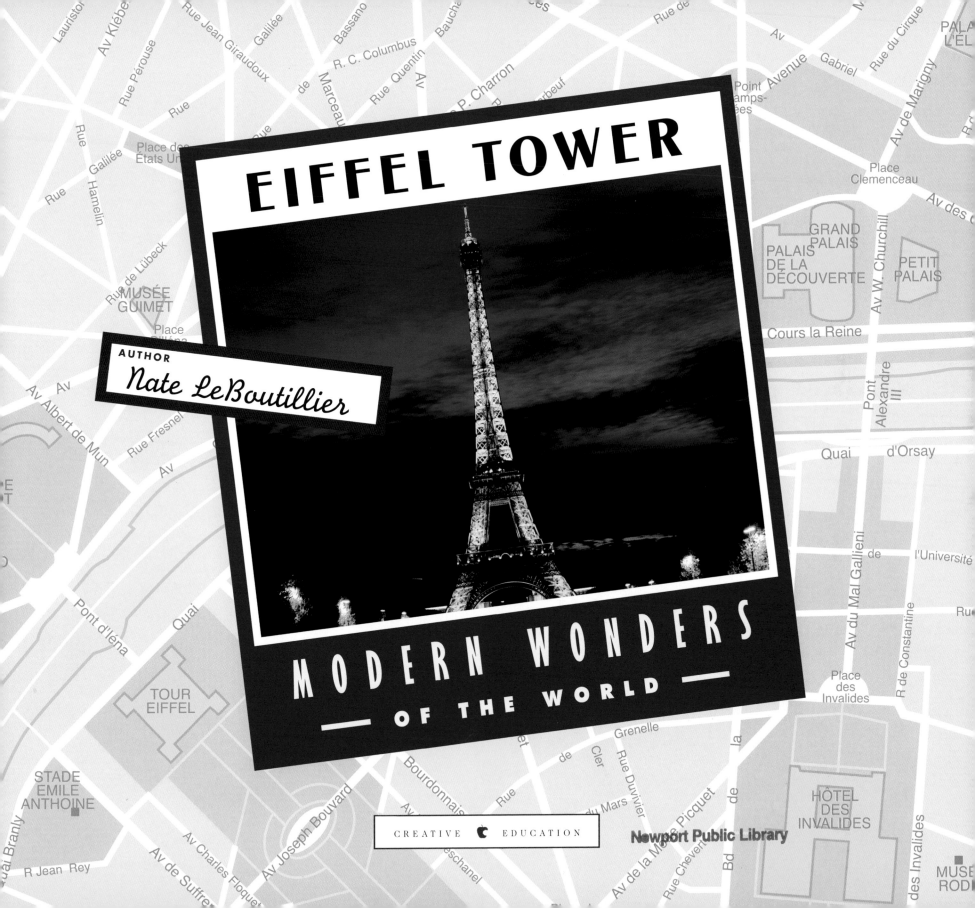

EIFFEL TOWER

AUTHOR
Nate LeBoutillier

MODERN WONDERS
— OF THE WORLD —

CREATIVE EDUCATION

EIFFEL TOWER

As much a work of art as a building, the Eiffel Tower rises regally from the heart of Paris, its majestic form visible around the city—and recognized around the world.

People in Paris, France, see it everywhere. The Eiffel Tower—*Le Tour Eiffel*, as the French call it—soars above the city's skyline, visible from so many angles. From the saintly outlook of the Sacre Coeur (Sacred Heart) cathedral, it rises, cutting in half the painting-of-Paris view. From the banks of the River Seine to the street-level vantage points of Paris's sidewalk cafés, it looms. From practically anywhere in Paris, if a person tilts the chin just right, he or she can see the Eiffel Tower. People who climb the elegant structure to take in the **panoramic** view of Paris feel what the visionaries behind the tower intended them to feel—man 1,000 feet (305 m) above ground, looking down.

A TALL ORDER

Although the Washington Monument (right) was the tallest structure in the world at the time it was built, it would soon be eclipsed by the Eiffel Tower, designed to serve as the entranceway to the 1889 Universal Exposition of the Products of Industry (opposite).

The Eiffel Tower was built near the end of the 19th century, a time when France needed a boost. In 1870, Germany had humiliated France in the Franco-Prussian War, throttling the French Imperial Army of Napoleon III. Paris itself had been under a five-month siege during the war, and 20,000 Parisians had died. People became so desperately hungry that some killed zoo animals for food.

Politically, France was a mess after the war. But a new French government called the Third Republic finally emerged in 1875. Among its early decisions was to hold a Universal Exposition of the Products of Industry in 1889. The Exposition, to take place in Paris, was open to other countries around the world as an opportunity to show off the latest technological inventions and share ideas. The Exposition would also mark the **centennial** of France's 1789 revolution and give the city of Paris a source of pride.

The people of Paris, and all of France, tried to think of a way to impress the world. There had been some talk in the years prior of building a great tower. England had considered a tall tower for London, and the United States was thinking the same for Philadelphia. In 1884, the U.S. built the 555-foot (168 m) Washington Monument in Washington, D.C. Finally, in May 1886, Edouard Lockroy, the

The **Panama Canal** Company went bankrupt in 1888 and accused Gustave Eiffel—who signed on to help with the **locks** on the canal—of misusing money. Eiffel eventually cleared his name and avoided a two-year jail sentence. He never worked on a large project again after the Eiffel Tower.

French minister of commerce and industry, declared a contest for **architects** and **engineers** to design a 1,000-foot (305 m) tower for the 1889 Exposition.

Contestants submitted a variety of proposals, including one that called for a tower built like an enormous watering can that would water Paris in the event of a drought. Another called for a tower with mirrors at the top reflecting light so bright that Paris would never be dark. But in the end, an engineer named Gustave Eiffel submitted the winning plan. Eiffel won the contest largely because his **blueprint** was one of the simplest and cheapest. His design featured four sturdy

base pillars that eventually joined together to make a slender but sturdy tower like an iron arrow thrusting into the sky.

The Exposition committee dilly-dallied on approving the construction until mid-1886, leaving less than three years to build the tower. Yet if one man was qualified to take up the task, it was Eiffel. The engineer had recently invented a complicated new method of building bridges using iron, and his detailed plans were not only **innovative**, they were efficient. For Paris's tower, Eiffel had to pick a building material that wouldn't topple because of weight, but would be strong enough to endure wind, rain, snow, and heat. He chose

8

By the time Gustave Eiffel (opposite) submitted his plan for Paris's tower, he had worked his way up from an entry-level position with a company that designed railway bridges to owner of a construction firm. Although the design he proposed for the Exposition's tower was simple, it featured beautifully detailed metalwork.

Guy de Maupassant, commonly regarded as France's best short story writer, was a chief objector to the Eiffel Tower. Bitterly, he ate his lunch at a restaurant inside it every day, saying, "It is the only place in Paris where I don't have to see it." Eventually, he moved away from Paris, blaming the tower.

a kind of iron that resembled the iron he used in his bridges. The worksite for Eiffel's tower opened on Paris's *Champ de Mars* (Martial Field) area, an old military parade ground, in July 1887.

Not everyone was happy about the tower's construction. Forty-seven prominent Parisians—including writers Alexandre Dumas and Guy de Maupassant and painter Charles Gounod—protested with a letter sent to Lockroy. Arguing that the tower would ruin the graceful Paris skyline, their letter began:

Writers, painters, sculptors, architects, passionate lovers of the heretofore intact beauty of Paris, we come to protest with all our strength, with all our indignation, in the name of betrayed French taste, in the name of threatened French art and history, against the erection in the heart of our capital of the useless and monstrous Eiffel Tower....

Lockroy responded by saying that the protest didn't come in time. The work had already started. Next to the ancient waters of the River Seine, the four base pillars were going into the ground on the *Champ de Mars*. The tower was going up.

Guy de Maupassant (opposite far left) was among those who feared that the Eiffel Tower would ruin the beauty of Paris, which was known for such stunning structures as the fountain in the Place Saint Sulpice (opposite center), the Fontaine de Medicis (top), the Opera (bottom left), and the Sacre Coeur (bottom right).

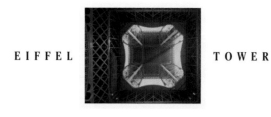
INTO THE SKY

Gustave Eiffel's nickname in France is *Le Magicien du Fer*, which means "The Magician of Iron." From photographs, Eiffel seems to be well-built, like the structures he created, but smallish—much unlike his structures. He was always well-dressed and rarely appeared without his top hat. Eiffel was in his mid-50s when the tower was built. By then, he had a large and distinguished body of work, including bridges in Portugal, Vietnam, and Algeria, as well as the dome of the Nice Observatory in France.

Paris's tower was unlike any other project that Eiffel had undertaken because it wasn't necessarily practical. The argument could be made that France needed the tower to restore a measure of confidence in the country itself, but other than for looks and pure fascination, some wondered what the tower would be used for. Eiffel seemed to be aware that if his tower did not serve more than just a fanciful purpose, it could be torn down someday. He said that he planned to conduct scientific experiments from the top of the tower, and, eventually, he would.

Awestruck Parisians stared at the worksite where the tower was emerging, piece by iron piece. But in October 1887, the approximately 200 laborers at work on the tower had to cease construction. A nervous gentleman who feared the tower

When the creator of the Statue of Liberty, Frederic Auguste Bartholdi, struggled in figuring out how to make the statue lighter, he consulted the "Magician of Iron," Gustave Eiffel, in 1881. Eiffel devised a lightweight but sturdy iron framework that keeps Lady Liberty standing tall today.

Parisians who objected to the Eiffel Tower used their best insults. They called it a "truly tragic street lamp," a "mast of iron gymnasium apparatus, incomplete, confused and deformed," and "a half-built factory pipe."

Since the Eiffel Tower's creation, artists have reproduced its beauty in paint, neon lights (far right), and even chocolate (right).

might fall onto his house brought a lawsuit against Eiffel and the city of Paris. The city refused to take responsibility should such an accident occur, and finally Eiffel agreed that if the tower fell, he would bear the blame.

In addition to making sure that the tower would be sturdy and level, Eiffel wanted his structure to look artistically captivating. There were to be three platforms for observation, and after the lowest of the three levels was finished in March 1888, it was evident that the structure held a certain elegance. The arches spanning the facing of the first level's platform were gracefully curved and pleasing to the eye. After completion of the second level, Eiffel held a rally for newspapermen on France's Bastille Day on July 14. The event spread the latest news of the tower's progress to the public.

Working on the Eiffel Tower was a tough job, with winds gusting colder and wilder the higher up the work went. The laborers spent most of their time hoisting and fitting Eiffel's carefully measured beams together and then hammering hot bolts called rivets into place, all while perched on elevated wooden

Although he threatened to reduce it to ruins during the Nazi invasion of Paris in 1940, German dictator Adolf Hitler may have secretly admired the Eiffel Tower. Born the same year as the tower, Hitler never scaled it, but posed for a photo in front of it.

Had Hitler (right, third from left) destroyed the Eiffel Tower, the view from the River Seine (opposite) would be very different today.

platforms. Eiffel had an elevated **canteen** built where workers could get their meals, making extra up-and-down climbing unnecessary.

Pay rates for the Eiffel Tower's builders ran from about 8 to 14 cents an hour. On September 19, 1888, workers put down their tools in a strike to demand a raise. Eiffel agreed to a small pay increase, and work went on without a hitch. When the tower's structure was completed in March 1889, Eiffel had the names of 199 workers who saw the whole job through painted on one of the tower's beams, visible to all.

On March 31, 1889, Gustave Eiffel and two of his highest-ranking workers invited a party of Exposition officials to climb the finished Eiffel Tower. Most of the men stopped at the first or second level, but Eiffel and a few others continued all the way to the top, taking half an hour to cover the more than 1,500 steps. There they raised the red, white, and blue French flag on a post. When they descended, the mood was one of celebration, and Eiffel gave a **patriotic** speech as the men cheered, shouting, *Vive la France!*—long live France!

THE GREAT LADY OF IRON

When the Exposition opened on May 5, 1889, the Eiffel Tower was the star of the show. The public stared in awe but had to wait to scale the tower until Eiffel and city officials were certain it could hold the weight of the many people eager to climb it all at once. When it finally opened on May 15, Parisians and world travelers alike took to the tower with gusto.

In the first week, nearly 50,000 people paid either 40 cents to walk up 189 feet (58 m) to the first level or 60 cents to continue to the second level, 380 feet (116 m) up. What they saw was a from-the-clouds view of Paris's famous sprawl, a view that until then had been enjoyed only by high-flying birds. The Exposition remained open a week after its planned closing date of October 31, 1889, and in the tower's first year, more than two million people paid for a visit.

Until his death in 1923 at the age of 91, Gustave Eiffel carried out experiments from the top of his tower. He studied weather conditions and published his findings. He dropped objects from the tower, recorded their speed, and connected this information to studies in aviation. He also installed a radio antenna that could transmit much farther than others

18

Gustave Eiffel (opposite, at left) could look down on the beautiful buildings and fountains of the 1889 Exposition (left) from the Eiffel Tower's spiral staircase, which led to his top-floor office. Brazilian Alberto Santos Dumont (below) found a new way to reach such heights— in 1900, he flew his dirigible, or airship, around the tower.

CHOCOLAT „GROOTES"

The Eiffel Tower is truly a wonder of iron. Its weight is so evenly distributed that it exerts about the same weight on the ground as a man sitting in a chair. One of the reasons the tower is so sturdy is that it is full of holes, allowing the wind to blow straight through it.

of the time, furthering technology in the study of radio waves. For 40 years, until the 1,046-foot (319 m) Chrysler Building was built in New York City in 1929, the Eiffel Tower was the world's tallest man-made structure.

Although the Eiffel Tower belongs to the city of Paris, a company called the Société Noevelle d'Exploitation de la Tour Eiffel (SNTE) has been in charge of the tower's operation since 1980. The SNTE launched a major **restoration** program on the Eiffel Tower in 1981 in which safety features were updated, faster elevators were installed, and some beams of iron that had twisted over the years were straightened.

The tower has gone through much **maintenance** over the years, including 18 paint jobs. These days, it gets a new, 60-ton (54 t) coat of paint every five years. The tower has featured a variety of lighting schemes over the years. In the year 2000, lights were set up so that for 10 minutes, every night on the hour, the tower sparkled as if a swarm of fireflies had encircled it.

The Eiffel Tower has hosted many odd activities and events in its history. There have

Although the Eiffel
Tower lost its title as the
world's tallest structure to
the Chrysler Building
(opposite far left), it has
never lost its status as one
of the world's most ele-
gant buildings. Much of
the tower's appeal lies in
its open latticework,
which can be appreciated
up close from its elevators
(bottom).

The Eiffel Tower's second level has seen some crazy happenings. In 1968, a cow was hoisted up to the second level to promote dairy products. In 1977, American golfer Arnold Palmer drove a golf ball off of it. And in 1989, French tightrope walker Philippe Petit walked 800 yards (731 m) on a wire to the second level.

been hot-air balloon races around the tower. One man rode his bicycle all the way down the tower's steps; another man hopped on one leg all the way up. There have been bungee jumpers, tightrope walkers, and political protesters. Crazy-hearted people have run nude on the tower, and more than a few have shared kisses or proposed marriage. On the dark side, the Eiffel Tower has seen many suicides, with people leaping from observation decks to their deaths.

In 1989, the 100th anniversary of the Eiffel Tower, 5.6 million people paid to visit the grand structure. In 1999, a record

6,368,534 people bought a ticket. In 2005, a giant sign bearing the Olympic logo was suspended from the tower's first level as part of an ultimately unsuccessful effort to lure the 2012 Games to Paris.

The Eiffel Tower is arguably the world's most famous monument, visited by millions of people from around the world and instantly recognized by millions more. The unique iron structure has become synonymous with Paris, and whether viewing it from a Paris locale, from the top of the tower itself, or in a photograph or film, people recognize it as it stands today, as stable and proud as ever.

L'INVENTEUR D'UN PARACHUTE, VOULANT EXPÉRIMENTER SON APPAREIL
SE JETTE DE LA PREMIÈRE PLATE-FORME DE LA TOUR EIFFEL ET SE TUE

Each year on Bastille Day, crowds gather at the Eiffel Tower for a spectacular fireworks display. Over the years, people have also gathered there to observe hot-air balloon races and tests of new inventions, including a parachute coat (above).

SEEING THE WONDER

Those wishing to see the Eiffel Tower first-hand in all its majesty must travel to Paris, France. Once visitors are in Paris, the tower can be reached by car, bus, or metro (subway). The tower is located on one end of a grass and gravel tree-lined expanse called the *Champ de Mars*, which stretches to the *Ecole Militaire* (military school) on the other end.

Many people (and pigeons) flock to the Eiffel Tower year-round. There are three levels to reach, the first being the cheapest and the third being the most expensive. Walking or taking an elevator affects the price, as does age. As of 2006, the price of tickets ranged from about 3 to 11 euro ($3–11 U.S.) per person.

Besides its world-famous views, the Eiffel Tower hosts a variety of attractions and services. On the first level is a snack bar, a post office, a small theater, Internet stations, historical displays, and a souvenir shop. The second level offers the best vantage point from which to take photographs in all directions. The third level features a representation of Gustave Eiffel's office, with wax figures of inventor Thomas Edison (one of the most famous early visitors to the tower) and Gustave Eiffel himself.

2 6

On December 28, 1895, some six years after the Eiffel Tower was raised, brothers Auguste and Louis Lumiere held the world's first public film screening in Paris. In the many films shot in Paris since then, the Eiffel Tower has made count-less appearances.

While wind may bother tourists, it doesn't hurt the masterfully constructed Eiffel Tower. Visitors should be aware, however, that if it's breezy on the ground, it will be even more blustery at the top of the tower, which can sway nearly three inches (7.5 cm) in a strong wind.

The summer months of June, July, and August are the most popular time of year to visit, but the Eiffel Tower is open year-round. In France, summers are hot, winters are cold, and spring and fall can bring windy, unpredictable weather; visitors are urged to dress appropriately and to be aware that winds blow more forcefully the higher one goes. From June 11 to August 29, the tower's operating hours are from 9:00 A.M. to 12:45 A.M.; the rest of the year, hours are from 9:30 A.M. to 11:45 P.M.

There are countless sights to see in close

proximity to the Eiffel Tower, most notably the world famous Louvre Museum (home of the *Mona Lisa* painting). Many renowned landmarks can be seen from the tower, including the *Arc de Triomphe* (a monumental arch), the Trocadero Gardens, and Passy Cemetery. It has been said that the most gorgeous views from the tower are available at twilight, but this is a matter of personal preference. Clear, sunny days allow for the farthest view, while a nightfall ascent can provide a glittering vista of the entire, illuminated city of Paris.

By far the tallest building in Paris, the Eiffel Tower offers breathtaking views of the beautiful Arc de Triomphe *(top, at center),* the lush Trocadero Gardens *(bottom), and the whole of Paris, making it the perfect location from which to behold France's great "City of Light."*

EIFFEL  TOWER

QUICK FACTS

Location: Paris, France

Time of construction: January 1887 to March 1889

Opening date: March 31, 1889; the opening celebration was attended by 400 journalists and featured the unfurling of the French flag and a 21-gun salute

Composition: Iron

Engineer: Gustave Eiffel

Work force involved: 300 laborers

Height: 986 feet (300.5 m) in 1889; 1,063 feet (324 m) after the addition of a television antenna in 1959

Height of observation levels: 189 feet (57 m); 380 feet (116 m); and 906 feet (276 m)

Weight: 11,130 tons (10,100 t)

Area covered: 2.54 acres (1 ha)

Number of steps: 1,665, from ground level to the top

Cost to build: $1.4 million (7.8 million gold francs)

Funded by: The French government and profits made from tourism

Visitors per year: ~ 6.2 million

architects — people who design buildings and other structures and oversee their construction

blueprint — a drawing or other image that shows a detailed plan of action; a model

canteen — a snack bar or small cafeteria

centennial — a 100th anniversary or a celebration of the anniversary

engineers — people skilled at designing buildings or public works

innovative — ahead of the times; describing something unlike anything done or created before

locks — sections of a waterway closed off with gates, in which ships are raised or lowered by adjusting the water level of that section

maintenance — upkeep; the work of keeping something in proper condition

Panama Canal — a man-made waterway created from 1904 to 1914 through the Central American country of Panama to connect the Pacific and Atlantic Oceans

panoramic — describing an unbroken view of an entire surrounding area

patriotic — inspired by love for or devotion to one's country

restoration — the act of bringing an object or process back to its original condition

INDEX